THE CANADIAN BRASS
TRUMPET CHRISTMAS DESCANTS

T0039499

ARRANGED BY LLOYD LARSON

2 Angels We Have Heard on High

2 Away in a Manger

3 The First Noel

3 Go, Tell It on the Mountain

4 Good Christian Friends, Rejoice

4 Hark! The Herald Angels Sing

5 It Came Upon the Midnight Clear

5 Joy to the World

6 O Come, All Ye Faithful

6 O Come, O Come, Emmanuel

7 O Little Town of Bethlehem

7 Once in Royal David's City

8 Silent Night

8 We Three Kings

8 What Child Is This?

Visit the official website of The Canadian Brass:
www.canbrass.com

HAL•LEONARD®
CORPORATION

7777 W. BLUEMOUND RD. P.O. BOX 13819 MILWAUKEE, WI 53213

Copyright © 2001 by HAL LEONARD CORPORATION
International Copyright Secured   All Rights Reserved

Visit Hal Leonard Online at
www.halleonard.com

ANGELS WE HAVE HEARD ON HIGH

Traditional French carol, 18th C.

Traditional French melody, 18th C.

Repeat as needed (opt.)

50484041

The Canadian Brass Christmas Carols - 2

Trumpet Descant
in B♭

AWAY IN A MANGER

Unknown author vs. 1 and 2
John Thomas McFarland vs. 3

James R. Murray, 1887

Repeat as needed (opt.)

50484041
The Canadian Brass Christmas Carols - 3

Trumpet Descant
in B♭

4

THE FIRST NOEL

Traditional English carol

Traditional English carol

Repeat as needed (opt.)

GO TELL IT ON THE MOUNTAIN

Words by John W. Work, Jr.

African-American Spiritual

Copyright © 2001 by HAL LEONARD CORPORATION

GOOD CHRISTIAN FRIENDS, REJOICE

Medieval Latin carol

IN DULCI JUBILO
Traditional German melody, 14th C.

HARK! THE HERALD ANGELS SING

Charles Wesley

Felix Mendelssohn

IT CAME UPON THE MIDNIGHT CLEAR

Edmund H. Sears

Richard Storrs Willis

STANDARD VERSION

Flowing (♩. = ca. 52)

Repeat as needed (opt.)

JOY TO THE WORLD

Isaac Watts

ANTIOCH
George F. Handel

Repeat as needed (opt.)

**Trumpet Descant
in B♭**

O COME, ALL YE FAITHFUL

**Latin hymn,
attributed to John F. Wade**

**ADESTE FIDELES
John F. Wade's Cantus Diversi, 1751**

**Trumpet Descant
in B♭**

O COME, O COME, EMMANUEL

Latin hymn, 12th C.

**VENI EMMANUEL
based on Plainsong**

O LITTLE TOWN OF BETHLEHEM

Phillips Brooks

ST. LOUIS
Lewis H. Redner

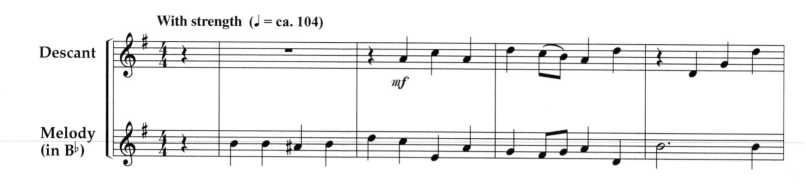

Repeat as needed (opt.)

50484041
The Canadian Brass Christmas Carols - 12

ONCE IN ROYAL DAVID'S CITY

Cecil F. Alexander

IRBY
Henry J. Gauntlett

SILENT NIGHT

Joseph Mohr

**STILLE NACHT
Franz Gruber**

Trumpet Descant
in B♭

WE THREE KINGS

John H. Hopkins, Jr.

KINGS OF ORIENT
John H. Hopkins, Jr.

50484041
The Canadian Brass Christmas Carols - 15

**Trumpet Descant
in B♭**

WHAT CHILD IS THIS?

William C. Dix

GREENSLEEVES
Traditional English melody, 16th C.